Slowing Down
  The Light
The Way

Slowing Down
The Light
The Way

LINDSEY HANNAHAN

MOBILE ALABAMA

Slowing Down   The Light   The Way

Copyright © 2020, Lindsey Hannahan
All rights reserved.

Cover Art by Lindsey Hannahan
Book Design by Jenni Krchak

ISBN 978-0-942544-07-7
Library of Congress Control Number: 2019934546

Negative Capability Press
150 Du Rhu Dr, #2202
Mobile, Alabama 36608
(251) 591-2922

www.negativecapabilitypress.org
facebook.com/negativecapabilitypress

For my husband Patrick,
For my daughters Mary Lindsey, Claudia, and Grace,
thank you for gifting me time, support
and space to write this book.

For my parents Claudia and Bob,
thank you for providing a home where
we were well-guided, secure and cherished.

Contents

Nature, Faith And Fortitude

Slowing Down The Light The Way	
and Conscious Decisions	3
Lord of All	4
Japanese Maple	5
Room For Growth	6
Whoever Drinks The Water Will Never Thirst	7
I Fell in Love With A Redbird	8
In Morning's Newness	9
In Spirit and Flames	10
Desert Blossoming	11
Tranquility's Cup	12
Something There is	13
Before They Fade	14
Beyond Ourselves	15
Messengers	16
Cleaning House	17
Lawn Party (Dance With Beyond)	18
Dawn's Doe	19
Voiceless	20

Two Tree Squirrels: Gardening	21
Indigo Garden Indeed	22
Treasure From The Hallowed Deep	23
Savoring Silence	24

Light Is Everything

Starlight in my Eyes	27
Battle Prayer	28
Filled With Light	29
Step Out of Shadows	30
Star-filled Days of Advent	31
The Lulling Melody	32
I Hunger	33
Quiet Quest	34
Untold Felicity	35
The Greater Distance	36
A Great Actress	37
And Then	38
Sing A New Song	39
Sacred Fruit: Bones, Breast, Breath Consumed	40
Morning Glory Matters	41

Take In, Take All, Take Hold

Take In, Take All, Take Hold	45
Southern Cordiality	46
As We Wander and Unwind in Mobile's Garden	48
Fairhope: The Wide Bay Breathes	49
Hearing With My Heart: Contemplative Retreat at Beckwith	50
Day Dawns in Point Clear	51
Be Here And Now: Grayton Beach	52
Little Beach Bird	53
Sea to Shining Sea	54
For Keeping: Alys Beach	55
Late Martin on an Autumn Afternoon	56
Darlington Refuge	57
Puttin' On Airs	58
Pine Barron Lake	
In Other Words: Escape	59
On the Way to Beaver Pond	60
Dinner for Three	61
I Want To Be There Again	62
Spreading Sunset	63

Enlightened To Perceive

Power Source	67
Dwell In Possibility	68
Truth Seeking	70
In His Presence Revival	71
Forsaken: This I Know	72
Holy Cry	73
Opus. Composition. Book.	74
Bride of Christ	76
Necessary Neediness	77
Where Are You?	78
Just Breathe	79
Shadow Out My Window: Sedona, Arizona	80
Untethered	81
Ungrayed	
In Other Words	82
Lapping Pink	84
What Needs to be Purged from My Inner Wardrobe?	85
Tame the Tongue	86
Forty-Eight Hours	87
Passageway	88

How to Grow a Garden

For Example	89
Healed Hidden Hurts	90
360 Degrees	91
Why Wait?	92
Say Goodbye To Distractions	93
Present, Quiet, Fully Conscious	94
From Her Labyrinth	95
Forget the Old Song	96
Scent The Invitation	97
Hands Hold Voice	98
Found Fortune	99
Airborne	100
Night Blooming	101
Brimming Bouquet	102
Harvested	103
The Quality of Mercy	104
Out Of My Limitations Words Cascade	105
More Than Hours	106

Brought To Remember

Dad: Your Time, Your Patience, Your Rocklike Love	109
Ode to Mother	110
Missing Mother	111
Remembering Mother	112
Mother's Last Words	113
Mourning the Death of Deep Conversation (A Conversation with Myself)	114
I Drown in Blue Dawn	115
Homeplace	116
Moving Mother and Daddy Out of Our Childhood Home of 51 Years	118
On a Field of Fresh Clover	119
Husband-Best Friend	120
As Eventide Approaches	122
Home for A Swift Visit	124
Celebrate Claudia	125
Blessed by Grace	126
Mother's Advice on Choosing Close Friends	128
Could This Be True?	129
Unbroken	130
A Sweet Retreat	131

Dear Catherine	132
Playing Field	133
A Day That Can Be	134
Dauphin Island Family Morning	135
A Mix of Memory	136
On Sand Island	137
Acknowledgments	139

*i thank You God for most this amazing
day:for the leaping greenly spirits of trees
and a blue true dream of sky; and for everything
which is natural which is infinite which is yes*

*(i who have died am alive again today,
and this is the sun's birthday; this is the birth
day of life and of love and wings: and of the gay
great happening illimitably earth)*

*how should tasting touching hearing seeing
breathing any–lifted from the no
of all nothing–human merely being
doubt unimaginable You?*

*(now the ears of my ears awake and
now the eyes of my eyes are opened)*

- e.e. cummings

Nature, Faith And Fortitude

Nature reveals her secrets if you listen - Paula D'Arcy

Without Him, we see only competition and the saddest traffic on the stage.
- Alison Touster-Reed

Slowing Down   The Light   The Way and Conscious Decisions

I   Slowing Down: Orange Beach

Salt clings to my summer skin. My feet burrow in morning
sand as I listen to a melody of waves breaking shore
thinking I could stand here until nightbird's chant.
Calendar-thoughts steal serenity;
I toss them to the wind and watch them fade.
My mind clears of chatter.

II   Bring in the Light [1]

Sea oats stir nearby. A door opens within, and I hear
You whispering, "Get off the rollercoaster.
Shed the hurried way. Take time to gather seashells
and find Myself in you. I lose desire for selfishness, fast pace.
The tide turns.

III The way to make your life better is to make it worse first [2]

"Cast your yesterdays into the sea.
Catch a glimmer of present living.
New grace dawns with the sun."
Mindfulness blooms.

The Ordeal of flying non-stop [3]

Notes:
1. Kazim Ali, "Refuge Temple," *Poetry,* April 2017
2. Ira Wood, *You're Married to Her,* 2012
3. Yudhijit Bhattacharjee, "Epic Migrations," *National Geographic,* March 2018

Lord of All

Lord of tide

sun   wind   sky

earth

universe

everyone all

even when not claimed

Lord of fenced

persons

open us

Japanese Maple

        Summer closes her arms
      and soon her greenage is gone
  and the boats and the beaches become barren.

But I cannot miss her
carefreeness as I fall
                            into the approaching
                                arms of autumn,

           and cooler days
           and the crimson sea
                          of leaves animating
                          the lawn's monarch,

     most regal at onset
     of darkness, when her
                               moon-kissed leaves
                               hold hundreds of

            flames
           following
            me to
            sleep,
          filling my
            limbs
        with Spirit,
        willing my
   dreams to take wing.

Room For Growth

                                            I walk

thirsty, unafraid
                into pine woods

                                        I leave

thoughts
                that would upbraid

                                        I move

boldly
                giving ear to nature's speech

                                        I adjoin

naked trees
                beneath Pleiades

                                        I get lost

in easy breath
                fall awake unvague

                                      I find water

waiting
                alongside bream and bass

                                      I partake

new growth

Whoever Drinks The Water Will Never Thirst

No matter where you go, there you are. - Confucius

        I watch a mullet jump

      and listen to leaves sing,

    when without warning a cloud unfolds.

   I stand waiting on the dock.

       Ruminating in rainfall,

     I realize I've been

   running from myself

half my life.

      I drink Your tender raindrops.

    My yearning yields blossom.

   My sleeping passion stirs

and my feet stop.

I Fell in Love With A Redbird

Streaks of scarlet

lightening land

in the backyard morning

on flowerless branches

of an ancient oleander.

Chanting

agreeable arrangements

the kind you

hum to, the kind that spurs

early buds to open

and forget missing blooms.

In Morning's Newness

I shut my eyes in order to see. - Paul Gauguin

It's amazing how a simple night's sleep
can relieve yesterday's resentment,

how early morning's coolness on last
night's puffy face can override
the day before's tirade that brought

on the good cry which ungated pent-up
frustration damned by ill-communicative habits,

how sunlight blushing on the lone pink camellia's
January voice stretching from shade to decorate

desolate winter moves one to act on the well-known
realization that disharmony with another
has no place in todayness,

how this morning's two crested jays brighten
with blueness, greenness before breakfast

can establish a well-deserved apology
sparking the other to an immediate "I'm sorry"
in morning's newness.

In Spirit and Flames
(For Paula)

Red birds begin to reign every day where birds are baptized

in neighborhood gardens in Spirit and flames.

There have never been so many.

The weight of the last few weeks feels greater than my strength

and I think I will sag to the ground like the stem

of an unpruned hydrangea. Perhaps I will break.

The sky bleeds. The air breeds crimson reminders of His Presence.

On late Spring leaves, over well-traveled streets, in bushes

and branches with flowers lighting a mid-May pre-Christmas'

celebration as reverent rubies bless creation.

And who can resist the red-coated cheerleaders flitting about their

fiery business clapping the hours into passionate existence?

And who can remain disheartened when God sends His harmonious

army to gently enter saddened spaces?

Royal red redeemers spread wide their wings and proclaim:

"Nothing in life is ever wasted."

Desert Blossoming

I cared for you in the wilderness, in the land of burning heat. - Hosea 13:5

Dove in the wind

    Emerging from celestial sphere

        Scattering dust,

            Evidence of God's presence,

                Rewarding endurance:

                    Temptation in the desert

Blossoms weaving a crown

    Life-giving water for wanderers, weary

        On parched land, on sweltering sand

            Spark yet unbroken

                Spirit Divine

                    Offering rescue

                        Mirage?

Tranquility's Cup

My cup overflows. - Psalm 23:5

Today I drink crystal words

from nature's nurturing cup of tranquility.

Your counsel will guide me

teach me to control wayward energy

puttering in stagnant surf.

Faced with life's challenges

I shall be the bending willow;

I shall meet harsh reality

with the nectar that flows

from sterling beauty.

Something There is

Just another kind of out-door game. - Robert Frost

Something

there is

about a fast

boat ride

over vast water

that is both mellow

and exhilarating,

the sovereignty

of waves

and osprey

in her piousness

deem conversation

trivial

Before They Fade

Sunlight spills on the hydrangea bush

near my bedroom window.

White pom-poms atop raised

wooden stems explode.

I stand on a soft carpet gazing

at star-shaped flowers,

eyes wide with wonder.

They shake their lacy petals,

sway in morning's breeze

and wave me to come outside.

Opening the window, I say

I would love to join them

but I must stay inside

and write their fanfare.

Beyond Ourselves

On the corner

of Wisteria and Woodland

a rose bush has stopped short of blooming.

Stirring from a state of preoccupation

I stop and consider the situation,

knowing God wastes nothing,

certain it has more than

one purpose.

Messengers

A breech-born calf plays on the hillside.

A menhaden emerges from a pelican's mouth unscathed.

In hard rain, a pregnant spider carries her load to safety.

Jonah, ran from God, swallowed by a whale

then saved.

Cleaning House

He chunks debris
and dumps sand out of his house--
a ghost-crab gone mad.
When all is tidy, he flits sideways
on lightening legs and boxy body

with towering eyestalks
and exposed eyeballs
fixed on a half-eaten cracker
falling onto a toppled wine bottle.
He snags the snack with tight

triumphant claws waving
in the late afternoon air
as he lingers in the spilled brew.
I chuckle thinking to myself
that I often mimic him.

Lawn Party (Dance With Beyond)

People from a planet without flowers would think we must be mad with joy the whole time to have such things about us. - Iris Murdoch

Inhaling hallelujah on the sunlit lawn:
bluebells, buttercups, begonias, bergenias,
twirl, twist, turn, tap shoes on.

Daisies, daffodils, dahlias, delphinium,
disco into day with jasmine, gardenia.

Pansies, peonies, poppies, plumerias,
prance in paws of Labrador Retriever.

Sparrow kicks up dirt; squirrel shakes her skirt.
Pine cones pirouette to drunken bougainvillea.

Robin rocks his head. Lavender, lilies, lilacs laugh.
Tipsy tulips two-step with a beagle ballerina.

Raccoons rollick. Crepe Myrtles frolic.
Honey suckle circles leaves of magnolia.

Turtles, frogs kiss, parade. Staggering feet sashay.
Petals, tepals, sepals, rhumba with satsumas.

Wisteria waltzes weeping willows;
butterflies bow, bounce, billow.
Pink, purple, white, red, yellow cut loose on green.

Dawn's Doe

The doe arrives before sun
touches the horizon leaving a trail
of hearts in the ground behind her.
She moves from a pine canopy to field's edge

searching for kin;
seeing safety in company,
she walks in to feed donning a dress
of camouflage darkened by winter months.

Her body bends to earth, her face blended
with the wild red berries she seeks.
She startles, looking up
with eyes full of stars and unease

scanning for predators,
with ears, triangles alert
and twisting as acorns
plummet to dirt.

When satisfied of no danger,
she swishes her tail,
sweeps it side to side
beckoning her ten-point love.

Voiceless

God is Beauty. - St. Francis of Assisi

Who can say there is no God
when encountering a Rosy Maple Moth?
Who can lack belief when staring
at the petite body of golden tweed:

a cashmere sun, a hundred hues
of heat, perfect legs of Persian pink
and made-to-match wings
by creation's Couturier

rendering a lover of words
voiceless with sunpinkfever.

Two Tree Squirrels: Gardening

scurry across branches

      plunder and horde forbidden figs

    go nuts in victory jumps, loop

        a Ferris wheel of twig and vine debris

            head down into shrubbery

        complete a little gardening

        then flee.

Indigo Garden Indeed

    A wasp with phantom wings builds

its honeycomb home.

    Two turtles love on the lawn.

    Red roses glow

beside a fruitless blueberry bush.

    One rose tilts its Cupped bloom.

    What is whispered in conversation?

What compassion found in curving petals

    as morning displays an indigo-blue garden.

Treasure From The Hallowed Deep

Diamonds prance on small waves
under an azure sky

the gateway
opening from salty deeps

a Snowy Egret rises from a buried chest
and releases plentiful pearls

Catch one
Ingest it

before sun's insistence
carries brilliance away.

Savoring Silence

Outside in darkness with mug of coffee

grateful for non-rushing minutes

Upraised mug salutes blackbird

pink petals' budding.

Light Is Everything

I will love the light for it shows me the way, yet I will endure darkness because it shows me the stars. - Og Mandino

Light is more than the sun. - Mary Oliver

Starlight in my Eyes

I remember and no longer cry
over past should-haves, mistakes, and failures.
Within, there is peace and starlight in my eyes

desiring to share my epiphanies; at the least, willing to try.
As a lover of persons, lover of being, with its array of peaks
and pressures, as I attempt to be an exhilarator,
I remember and no longer cry.

When my time on earth is complete and God opens the sky,
don't fret my daughters three, precious pleasures,
within, there is peace and starlight in my eyes.

I have lost and been lost as if in an endless good-bye.
I have loved and been loved, my foremost treasures.
I remember and no longer cry

though raindrops, like tears, drip from the weeping willow's sigh
though clouds grumble, tomorrow will bear buoyant weather.
Within, there is peace and starlight in my eyes.

Let's throw a party and dance onstage; on the swing-set, let's go high.
Let's celebrate pastpresentfuture without measure.
I remember and no longer cry.
Within, there is peace and starlight in my eyes.

Battle Prayer

For the battle is not yours, but God's. - 2 Chronicles 20:15

Strengthen my fighting heart

in its war against the mountains

of doubt that loom before

diminishing faith.

Save me from compromise,

chain reactions and dull habits

so I can follow on undivided

realizing calm laughter.

Solidify deep desire

with new hope to bestow

my blaze of light, my worship

my certainty.

Filled With Light

Breathing stops for a moment.

Feet, as if clay.

Eyes freeze upon seeing

thousands of saffron leaves

flutter as if winged.

Have I stumbled upon

a butterfly garden beside

the persimmon tree?

Energy flows between us.

Joy grows here, where gingko

take their grand golden stand.

We are full of light.

Overnight foliage flies to earth

in synchronized acceptance.

Morning's gold

beneath my feet.

Step Out of Shadows

which devour light

      and blend day, night

           into an albatross of steel gray

                  binding the frozen soul to gloom.

Star-filled Days of Advent

We saw his star at its rising. - Matthew 2:2

Among dazzling houses, holiday music
shopping for trinkets to fill
stockings   bags   boxes
red   white   golden   silvery   ornaments

delighting in Christmas green,
cookies   candy   cakes   cocktails
and festivities to make merry days
lay Advent's star.

And perfect parties, perfect trees
perfect purchases   decorations   recipes
will fatten believers for only a short season
unless we empty ourselves to crown room for Him,

reflect on the nativity's relevance
and inspect our lives, ready our hearts
to prevail with Love Incarnate
Realizer of God's promises.

Jesus   God   Man   King
Redeemer   Descender   Truth   Perfection

wrapped in rags glowing in a modest manger,
brings undying life to a dying world waiting wearily
for the Savior to erase estrangement from God

to walk with us on this grandbrokenuncertainearth
open Heaven's borders and feed
our lives with contentment
the world cannot offer.

The Lulling Melody

Be still, and know that I am God. - Psalm 46:10

Beside the window as rain descends,

I unwind to the soulful sound.

With ears deep open, sight wide asleep

I enter the light stilled, serene.

God gifts me in the dull gray hour

in fidelity to silence my tired breath enlivens.

Despite lingering uncertainty,

I rise.

I Hunger

Spiritual poverty is the greatest disease. - Mother Teresa

like my dear Beagle Bella
devouring bread dropped
on the kitchen floor
when I just fed her a bowlful

like the Ground squirrel
I eyeballed this morning
mauling the Nutella cauldron.

Quiet Quest

    Listen to the flame within

        holy fire igniting

            blazing stillness

                speaking beyond bounds

    Passionate dance in the heart

        electricity in vein

            no energy expended

                here God speaks your name

Untold Felicity

One word frees us from all the weight and pain of life. That word is love.- Sophocles

Living

difficult   frightening

unfair   violent

full of yearning   hunger   hatred   heartbreak

drudgery   labor

crumbled   dreams

thrilling   inspiring

festive   fulfilling

full of felicity   virtue   valor   beauty

blessings   encouragement

heroism   love   light

The Greater Distance

He declared the end from the beginning. - Isaiah 46:10,11

Disappointment topples trust.

A black sun rises.

Despair climbs in bed with bitterness.

Anger fulfills its assignment.

Surrender it to God

who sees the greater distance.

There is starlight in the fog

to guide you to water.

A Great Actress

He who follows me shall have the light of life. - John 8:12

A quiet sun hides reality.
Having much practice

with well-rehearsed answers;
tears dry and pleasant

but behind dim rays
sadness lies scared.

"All is fine."
Pretend blithe surety.

Today's demands, due
process denied,

the whirlwind of faces must
be encountered.

Repaint happy.
Makeup face.

Murder fatigue.
Seek Light.

And Then

Ponder: the pear tree no longer producing.

Consider how we fail when we focus
all ardor on our own spiritual development.

Consider we were created to propagate
God-authored faith for more than our own flowering.

Consider our sources of light.
Acknowledge why famine has come.

Sing A New Song

In the cold of blackest gray
when the discourager slyly offers a trinket

do not succumb to silvery songs
whispering defeat

Rise
flee from the thief

Run
as the refugee into life

Remember
to speak God's sureties
certain night's power

Rest
in comfortable silence

Breathe
in sunrise and sing

I will make the Darkness
Light Before you*

I Will Make The Darkness Light - Alicia Keyes*

Sacred Fruit: Bones, Breast, Breath Consumed

Holy Mary
I feel
your spirit
enlist in
my distress,
your
reassuring
plea
intercede
on my behalf.
Mother of Christ, cry my tears, unite me in His name.
As you place my eyes on your Son, in his wounds
He holds me;
life-giving
blood flows.
I feel
three hearts
connected,
arms holding
me tight,
harmony
of Heaven
radiating light,
certain
love of Jesus,
Sacred Fruit:
bones, breast,
breath,
consumed.

Morning Glory Matters

*Whatever is true, noble, right, whatever is pure, lovely, admirable -
if anything is excellent or praiseworthy - think about such things. - Phil.4:8*

This morning the Glories
unfurl their parasols into full dress
before sun lifts her unconquered energy.

Twining vines full of vibrant flowers
trumpeting lyrics of first light.
Then the media blares its incessant
negative news and I ponder if its ok to smile--

a reminder to keep alive the practice of looking past
the flash floods of confusion inundating our places
to find and focus on what is right

true, praiseworthy, lovely, life-giving
opening the gift of wonderment,
keeping optimism vibrant before we fade
into our afternoon of life.

Take In, Take All, Take Hold

Thousands of Waving Hands, Take Hold. - Marge Piercy

The worst that can be said about a man is that he didn't pay attention.
                    - William Meredith

Take In, Take All, Take Hold

Why not take splendor
in September's stunning span
of sky's easeful blue

why not take in
take all
take hold
of water's soothing revenue—
the blue moon's pull
offering reflection,
measured meeting.

Why not grasp, capture
placidly carry forward
full meaning. Why not?

Southern Cordiality

Parties and piety

salty bay kisses

West Indies salad

seven historic districts

Bellingrath Gardens

twin tunnels

mild winters

blazing summers

Delta rich

deep-water port city

Battleship Memorial Park

boating, shrimping, fishing

Mardi Gras's birthplace

past preservation

Excelsior Brass Band jazz

city-wide celebrations

multifold museums

old oak canopies

Pollman's cookies, cakes

downtown Dauphin Street

thriving Arts

deeply-rooted communities

Dew Drop hotdogs

Carpe Diem coffee

Moon Pie Drop

Pride of Mobile Azaleas

oysters from Wintzell's

Jean-Baptiste LeMoyne, Sieur Bienville

My Mobile

As We Wander and Unwind in Mobile's Garden

As Mobile's new moon takes her broad breath and puts on her full face,
as autumn's leaves fall and darkness shines
as day in October's garden, aglow in fresh energy,
as we gather on benches among fountains of ferns, Dianthus, Salvias…

Let us unwrap opportunities to shed fullness of ourselves and step out
of our own keeping as we exhale the white-caps of yesterday and
wander among petaled reminders of our delicate state, resting atop
silvery stems as fingers point to our preferred phase.

As we get to know ourselves a bit better and realize how readily
we can be pulled apart from what most matters,
let us travel within a botanical harvest to reopen our horizons and dare
to discover that our deepest selves are precious.

As we delve not only into our own concerns but those of others
and decide not to debate but dash to help, as we marinate
in moon-night mystery and breadth in union with the universe and
sip from our garden's golden cup cradling us together,

as we rephrase who we are and return to tomorrow
as spacious vessels of combined sun-moon-fire, we are able
to contain earth's contradictions with courage and acceptance.
Let us delight in the moon-glow of our humanity.

Fairhope: The Wide Bay Breathes

From crowded houses,

    myriad boats,

        peopled throngs

            awaits excellence.

Shrouded waters

    renew sagging spirits.

        Rare beauty out-rivals

            elapsed best hours.

Quietude invites,

    reflection reigns.

        The wide bay breathes

            harmony with morning light.

Hearing With My Heart:
Contemplative Retreat at Beckwith

The dream of the toads rang through the elms by Little River and affected the thoughts of men, though they were not conscious that they heard it.
- Henry David Thoreau

Reverberations from the Meditation Bowl exude relaxing tones;
Weeks Bay waves beat against enormous rocks.

The music of a boat's engine inches into bottomless water;
I lean into being's present moment.

Leaves crumble under my feet while walking on Beckwith Lane
as a black snake rushes away in sodden grass

and a brown pelican plunges head first into the shallows.
Sounds of sacred silence surround me.

Toads stir in the shrubbery.
A Labrador's rhythmic pant joins prayer-chant muffles:
contemplative breaths

affirming mutual indwelling Presence; my mind:
knowledge of my deepest identity.

A bonfire sputters, keeping no-see-ums from reaching exposed skin.
A colony of gull's hungry screams search for a snack.

As wind passes through thin trees and well-cloaked evergreens,
I taste what I've been seeking.

Cardinals tap on the chapel window, then fly downward,
their whistled song flowing from the drab undergrowth,

I am, here now, in this: hearing with my heart.

Day Dawns in Point Clear

Outside walls, under a cerulean ceiling,
beside old Southern Oaks
a brown pelican dives into rich water
with full throat bag spilling breakfast
as heron laughs teasing a fiddler crab.

Cocker Spaniel pursues a duck duo
drinking from a sprinkler head
as white terns burst from sand and wing in.

I linger on the boardwalk hoping for a jubilee*
wishing not to leave and thinking
no need to travel to far-flung places
for picturesque scenery.

*Mobile Bay Jubilee- summer stunner
cinch to catch beached seafood
flounder, crabs, shrimp aplenty

Be Here And Now: Grayton Beach

Do you have eyes and not see, ears and not hear? - Mark 8:18

With fronds of palm
       the gusty wind dances amid
             pearls of holy sand romancing
                    gull and reed beside emerald waters
                          of Grayton Beach.

Over disquietude
       garnering retreat, idleness honors
             spiritual paths transcending
             measured words,
                     eyes mirroring the gift of see.

The bundled mind
       seldom perceives insight;
             refreshment needed.
                     Spinning past a dolphin duo
                           splashing, glowing red heavens
                               sea turtle tracks.

Missing connectivity:
       seaside's harvest.

Little Beach Bird

*Wagging its rear end
the sandpiper scurrying
sure amuses me.*

That little beach bird of unbleached color,

the one with long legs running

like a wound-up toy

stopping, starting every few feet.

The chick in the chestnut overcoat

searches the Gulf Coast

with her lengthy narrow black bill,

a quiet sewing machine flinging

sand, foraging deep, cruising

low over shallow water for a short time

on drawn-out pointed wings

until she blends again.

Weet-weet weet-weet

Sea to Shining Sea

        All week

                the waves

      of Sea Grove Beach

rise like mountains

      curl and dissolve

                into froth

                        scatter clear bubbles

                and swash

     around feet

then recede into water

       unleashing

             weightless

                    dreams.

For Keeping: Alys Beach

Dawn after dawn

sunlight

bejewels the body

of water

which bares

its shoeless closet

beside sleepy sand

its clothes

of greens

blues and earth tones

borrowed

with promise

its cloak

of pleasure peace

gemstones

a flawless

prayer.

Late Martin on an Autumn Afternoon

Late afternoon in the lakeside garden,
wind-song's waterfall of sound
carries me into a deep ground of contemplation.

I get lost in the energy of a bumble bee
prancing on pink peonies, loving on sunflowers,
kissing the golden lantana beneath the butterfly tree
and hugging the hibiscus in her immense social hours.

My gallery of intolerances takes off on wings of the bald eagle
as he swings over the garden, over the water, over the pine
trees of Smith Mountain with purple martins caroling
after him. A hummingbird watches

from orange blossoms as green snakes sunbathe
at the pollen party; as an eagle arrives again with expanded
entourage encompassing the sky and floating through the colossal
rainbow with feathers emptied of cargo.

Darlington Refuge

He must increase, I must decrease. - John 3:30

My soles sink into wet red clay;

    all that is still invites my entering.

        As crowded expressions lift without lingering,

            unrest bows to country miles deeper breath.

Solitude rises to clasp my hand;

    unknown capabilities feed into longest lengths,

        fueling unbroken gratitude's ungated peace.

            And I decrease, unceremoniously.

When pink blends into graying blue,

    city miles summon from refuge.

        With cool clay on palms, feet,

            my sound-soul takes lighter leave.

Puttin' On Airs

Now and then its good to pause in our pursuit of happiness and just be happy.
- Guillaume Apollinaire

"It's far too cold to venture outside this morning,"
said the weatherman. Yet here I stand freezing
in January's drizzle, watching the funfair.

Perhaps they're swallows or maybe hated starlings.
Too large to be purple martins.
It's difficult to distinguish the dark birds
rollercoastering above in the haze

as they dash, dart, dip, dance in figure eights
between well-clothed cedars, bare cypress
hackberry, ash and drop for muddy grub
in sky-diving madness,

moving on to flirt with carpe, bream, bass
and a game of chance
landing on an old gator's back.

They rocket over the lake, black flakelets on fire,
accomplished acrobats teasing, singing
while winging high fives.

My foot tapping, head bobbing, hands clapping
arms flapping; my body like the sun
resplendent on an Alabama August afternoon.

Pine Barron Lake
In Other Words: Escape

I steal beyond and fall into idle pace
into my modest sanctuary
to lie beside a country lake
for soft shoulder and rescued
breath's dare of introspection.

Flimsy thoughts walk away,
over browned crunchy leaves
around half-shadowed country trees
fertile roots breaking bread
in nature's small expansion.

With ease they evaporate
enabling my escape into generations
of country birds' congregation:
crow   heron   dove   drake
lording   turtle   bluegill   otter   snake
spawning ripples of rumination.

No tongue moves to interrupt
my sacred realm of honesty.
I float freely in my country breeze,
mind clear of artificial debris,
heart bowed, linked with companions.

Together we reverence,
uphold nature's revelations.

On the Way to Beaver Pond

Through an unseen spider web clinging to our camo and jeans,
through angry honey bees bursting from a hollow tree,
our hands in full combat,
exhausted and scratched from swatting them,

we keep walking

over crawfish holes and a dead oak limb's collection of fungi,
through the swampland in early March on the way to Beaver
Pond checking for last fall's buck-rubs and dormant scrapes,
dusting pits, feathers, flattened ground
and fence breaks to determine how yesterday's calf escaped.

We keep moving

past a broken concrete slab on the Wilcox-Butler County line
where the old seventies juke joint used to thrive.
We hear spitting and drumming.
There we see him showing off in sunlight.

We keep quieting

and still at the sight of a strutting gobbler
sporting a puffed-up vest,
fanning and flaunting eighteen stunning tail feathers
of iridescent bronze, copper and Christmas chroma
for nine hot-blooded hens encircling him,
fanning themselves but not from the sun.

Dinner for Three

Two thieving cormorants lick their lips
and flip down to dine in Lake Eufaula.
The lake is spry this evening
as shadows dance at twilight.
The spread for two lovers seems safe

on the picnic table though I spy
a thin fox-squirrel in an ill-fitting and rusty robe,
a black mask on his face as he races
across the deck railing, clucking and chucking.

He jumps at least fourteen impressive feet
and plunges into the birthday feast,
yelling as he gobbles. "I'm sorry.
I don't usually eat this sort of thing,
but I'm starving.

Earlier this week, someone stole my oak tree
and I cannot remember where
last week's nuts and acorns are stored."
This confession brings to mind the frustrating truth:
I cannot find where I placed

my diamond ring and recall the time I left
chicken cutlets in the Suburban's 95-degree heat.
I persuade my born-to-hunt husband
to lay aside his 22 and we join Mr. Fox.

I Want To Be There Again

driving over less-traveled highways
where the farmer from his tractor waves me
on past fertile fields of fluffy southern snow,
dilapidated and up-to-date silos

where fresh mown pastures and rows of round bales
lend awe and order to the crumbled rusty barn and downed
barbed-wire fencepost tangled in tough tassels,
verdant leaves and browned silky hair atop
ears bound in tight shucks,

where I feel audible praises flowing
from a roadside church, savor hand-arranged bouquets
from the neighboring yard of graves,

where the unafraid fox jogs and the racoon runs amuck
onto a gravelly county road and grassy driveway,

where cricket and crow are certain to have their say.
Wild flowers flourish January through December.
Cows curl tongues around crimson and Dutch White clover-
where donkey protects calf from coyote,

where alabaster birds light leafless pond tree branches,
the pregnant doe slurps from a nearby mudhole
stepping closer, and staring into my eyes nodding in amity,

where vanity's polished face vanishes beneath mistletoe
nesting solo in the Pin Oak,
where the massive sycamore shouts Glory Be.

Spreading Sunset

bringing winged gardens

tiny lantana smilers

splashing flowerbeds

colorful clusters

sweet-scented musical notes

send forth nourishment

the art of the Lord

who is working in all things

uplifts the lonely

Enlightened To Perceive

You don't have a soul. You are a soul. You have a body. - C. S. Lewis

If you are ever gonna learn to fly without fear, you've gotta learn to use those wings you cannot see. - Wings by Will Kimbrough

Power Source

Arise, take up your mat, and walk. - John 5:8

Rise

keep going

with feet that wish to cower

believe that God, all-knowing

all-powerful, all-loving

shall cover the day's hours

with His steadiness

so steps shall be firm

much lighter

and be empowered

to showcase

the Sovereign Supplier

Dwell In Possibility
(For Anna)

Where are we going with our lives?
We flirt with fear that opens
a hurricane of doubt blasting our pathways
nudging us to try new feelings-
like spring humming, dancing, sending invitations
from galaxies to Earth, to nature's animals, to all persons

that heightening happiness is possible if those persons
persist until fulfillment flows through their lives
as the universe extends its multifold invitations
to fly on earth's wing into Sirius' metallic arm that opens
us, tells us to dwell in possibility,*capture far-flung feelings
of glee. In what unique ways

might there be more valid realities? Don't follow others' ways
or imitate their actions to gain another person's
consent. Listen to how we may attend to our feelings
and ascend the ladder leading to lives
as victorious as wildflowers bursting open,
as salmon run to breed on gravel beds bearing invitation

to persevere in seasons of adversity and invitation
to live before we pass beyond and birth new ways;
make dreams realities that open
curiosities' potential and become persons
who seek and find fresh zest in lives
to questions of being and feelings.

How can we enrich our brief existence? Feelings
flow, ebb, then fade. God's opulent invitation
to uncover originality stands available to bless our lives
and dismiss discontent. Carpe Diem. Discover ways
to shine on monochromatic days, as persons
become true to themselves and hidden light opens

new careers, creative gifts as desire for philanthropy opens
our essence, our energy, our movement. Feelings
don't match experiences. Let us surround ourselves with persons
places, events that encourage and offer invitations
to inspiration without inflicting their ways.
Let us speak affirmations to nourish our lives

as intentional persons. Let us try a novel venture that opens
our tender, priceless lives, unleashes acute feelings
into alacrity, accepts God's invitations, overcomes stumbling ways.

* Emily Dickinson

Truth Seeking

The truth is incontrovertible. Malice may attack it. Ignorance may deride it, but in the end, there it is. - Churchill

Growth, Greenness, Grace

with eager salutation, heeded appreciation

outseek a quiet place, come to understand

its necessity to encounter empty spaces

and unobstructed views which perpetuate

distinguishable truth.

In His Presence Revival

(Backyard, early morning fellowship)

    The door opens
        silence broken
        mirror's reflection
            exudes expectation

    The morning invites
        oblation ignites
        robin's expression
            proposes reflection

    The seat chosen
        cloudscape rose-colored
        prayer unspoken
            kisses creation

    The proof unshaken
        joyance unmistaken
        camellia's beautification
            joins commendation

    The day widens
        the sun serenades.

Forsaken: This I Know

His appearance was so disfigured beyond that of any human being and his form marred beyond human likeness. - Isaiah 52:14

In a dreadful way, in a desolate place, in darkness
Jesus, Son of God, Sinless Soul
you gave up your life in untold torment
and lavish love for a world past hope,

endured, mockery, ridicule, rejection,
blood-sweat in the night, thorns embedded
grisly stripes, raw wounds, nailed hands and feet,
disfigured body of the living innocent

determined to drink Your cup full of every
sin committed and to be committed by man.
Feeling forsaken, questioning, yet trusting your Father
who must have cried out of love for you, for all His children.

Blessed Insurance of Eternal Life extinguished
for a short time on a hill called Golgotha.
I cannot grasp your suffering.
I try.

My distracted mind holds
focus and gratitude
for this greatest act.
My thoughts run to Your Resurrection.

Holy Cry
(For Pam)

The word of God is living and effective, sharper than any two-edged sword, penetrating even between soul and spirit, joints and marrow. - Hebrews 4:12

And I cried,
    joyful rivulets
        engraving my face; medicinal shards piercing
            each corridor of my heart.

And I began receiving,
    when I heard the bells pealing, burdens were lifted,
        transformation rooted as You
            breathed a concert of unabated grace.

And I cried,
    that crowded day I came alive,
        when I felt Your Word spoken, penetrating
            with unrestricted love and forgiveness.

And I began receiving,
    my boundaries' sovereignty, conceded
        miniature thinking overpowered,
            new eyes unblinded, undoubting.

And I cried.
    And I began receiving,
        and allowed You to breathe for me.

Opus. Composition. Book.

Alive again; he was lost and is found. - Luke 15:32

I hear the angels singing artful notes, the recurring symmetrical theme—

trumpet, tuba, tambourine, harmonizing inside of me

with sacred structure shaping poetic expression.

I hear the music.

I see my Heavenly Father running to welcome His obstinate daughter.

I see His lips forming my name with extraordinary tenderness.

I feel barricades breaking, pardon flooding my bloodstream,

unworthiness crawling into her tomb, love's anointing.

I feel compassion's cloak covering my brittle bones,

the warm kiss on my wetted cheek; my fingers let go shame's wings.

I touch the golden ring glimmering on my finger.

I touch truth within my limbs, arteries, muscles, brain chiming

"Our relationship was never severed."

I taste lobster, caviar, champagne - liberty dressing my homecoming table.

I taste newfound strength simmering in fattened meat.

I let go ego's tightening hand, step calmly on perfection's charming feet;

in new sandals, I dance with my Maker to the tantalizing tune

It Is Well With My Soul* pumping slightly left of center chest

on a slate swept clean.

*Horatio Spafford

Bride of Christ

As a lily among thorns, so is my beloved among women. - Song of Songs 2:2
He brings me to his banquet hall and his banner over me is love.
- Song of Songs 2:4

You have drawn me with loving kindness,
clothed me in mercy and compassion.
I know now, I am Your darling among maidens,
Your lily among thorns.

Yet as I get near You, Most Pure, Most Holy,
I hesitate, conscious of my sins beaming.
Yet you see me precisely, love me unconditionally
speak my name in adoration as You take my hand.

I must repent. I must be cleansed.
With face bathed in grateful tears,
I am loved into wholeness. I will go great lengths
to feel Your Presence—my heart's desire.

Yet I was Your heart's desire first, before time.
You waited with patience for me to receive Your grace
to stand as Your beloved bride,
to say I will follow you and mean it,

to walk down Your isle of grand love, arm in arm,
two Spirits infused at our banquet table.
You have autographed my heart,
branded my soul.

Necessary Neediness

Neediness never forsakes me.
Consistent companion, relentless reminder
I am wholly dependent on You God,
to live out my inheritance- the prolific life
You have prepared for me.

A catalyst to channel
leanings toward You.
For without them, tendencies are minimal:
devotion, prayer, acknowledgment
of Your presence, minimal living.

Autonomous spirit,
you induce my fall into bouts of isolation;
aloneness in the chaos.
For fellowship with my Father to be obtained,
maintained, you must wilt, die.

Blessed brokenness, conducive
for hunger to bloom (although at times,
I begged You to help me quickly; You knew better).
Here, credence conceived; boundless belief born.
Fruit of my poverty, deeper union with You.

Where Are You?

Where are you, faith?
Where are you, hope?
Your company is needed.
I know you dwell in me.
I beg you, make yourselves known.

Have you been suppressed by my own doing?

Though I have long lived as witness,
belief is teetering, patience flimsy.
I've stepped away again
and I'm sorry to have stepped
a broad distance.

Yet I cling to your sure definitions
and repeat them often,
*Faith is confidence in what we hope for
and assurance about what we do not see.
Hope does not disappoint.*

Where are you?

Just Breathe

An elephant sits on my chest

endeavoring to crush trumpets in my heart.

I gasp at immobility, remind myself to breathe,

opposing suffocation's sureness.

What can move the seemingly immovable?

I stir, stew, and reach beyond

from a perpetual position of hope.

Faith salutes in definitive response

to my expanding heart's chambers

opening, respiring, delighting

in remembered revelations

Elephants can fly.

Shadow Out My Window: Sedona, Arizona

Whether you like it or not, you are taking the information you get from watching TV and putting it in your brain. - Stephanie Beatriz

The shadow in the street

looks like the monster I saw

late last night on TV.

I wonder if I had not watched the show,

could the shadow evoke Sedona's

red-rock beauty?

Untethered

I begin this day aware
of what God has taken.
Before my feet touch the carpet,
my lips speak grateful prayer.

Before loved ones stir,
before bustling occurs,
before breakfast,
tiptoeing down dark stairs

morning's sweetness
lies in waking early, untethered.
It's no secret
what's not present in my spirit,

binding wrath, bitterness bulbs
endangering worry in seeking
approval of others.
Herein, a cage door opens.

Ungrayed
In Other Words

Color me happy
between lines
orderly and uncluttered
hypnotized for a time

With Eyes Wide Open*
to watch for better days
an edgy agenda
for one long-grounded gray

Out of twilight shadows
into lime's exhilarating green
essence of jubilance
laminates this scene

Glittering gold glazes
lemonluminous shades
bold bright bluepurplered
exploding on my page

Forsaking all colors fusty
no matter if in style
dressed iridescently
in resplendent rainbow smiles

Color me excessively
extroverted and bejeweled
courageously inoppressible
epitome of my real

Adorn me in insatiable cheer
bottomless supply of grace
with mouth mute to bland blue
no tear to sting my face

Hug me in humongous hope
tangibly pert and rad
dazzle my grief into overshrink
I plea gladness.

With Eyes Wide Open - In Flames

Lapping Pink

*George Lindley Taber
an old Southern favorite
showy azalea*

This morning

through the kitchen window,

azalea bushes bloom.

The first I've seen this early spring.

I run through the house

dismissing chores and

out the door to lap pink.

This evening

I'm sunburned and chirpy

awake until midnight

paying bills, washing towels,

bathing the dog, answering emails

in a George Taber world.

What Needs to be Purged from My Inner Wardrobe?

Jealousy is a mental cancer. - B.C. Forbes

Sparrow stops by
    for chat and coffee

I sing
I splash
I fling
    my flip flops from feet
        to shallows
we drink
we laugh
    until our cheeks hurt
     and our throats
      become hoarse

we hear
    a chickadee teasing
     from a palm tree
      her elegant black hat

    elevating her simple song,
      "Hey sweetie, Hey sweetie"

he caffeines over to her
    for a game of hide and seek
     leaving me lonely

my brown eyes greening.

Tame the Tongue

My tongue scatters

unflattering

words.

Taste buds sour.

Opportunity erased

to rise above.

Forty-Eight Hours

I organized all closets, drawers and cabinets,
merged my to-do lists; where is it?

I got it together, but then I lost it.

Completed persistent paperwork,
missed a turn on the way to Starbucks

I got it together, but then I lost it.

Left my credit card with the doctor's receptionist,
searched the parking lot for over ten minutes
(white cars must be very popular)

I got it together, but then I lost it.

Backed into my husband's truck in the driveway,
searched the house for my purse;
(found it with the laundry)

I got it together, but then I lost it.

Ran into myself endeavoring to get out the door,
called the butcher questioning laptop problems
(at least their names are Eric)

I got it together, but then I lost it.

Why is that car honking at me?
Does a yellow traffic light really mean yield?

I got it together, but then I lost it.

Passageway

Two faces stare

from the mirror

one   exhausted   impatient

and an idealist

the other   laughing   per diem

enjoying the mode

allowing innate pathway

to leaf

How to Grow a Garden
For Example

(for Mary Lou)

toss the browned flowers
into deep-rooted crevices,
hammer the hardest ground
with refreshing rain.

Let go long-held outworn thoughts.
Seed fresh florets
in clear waters of the gospel,
outshining shadows of doubt.

Give power to this holy hour's opening
the never-told crosses of ancient formation
and fly unbridled with the rain bird
into moonbows.

Healed Hidden Hurts

Listen to the advice of experience
telling you that your fossilized
feelings immersed in much-needed
meltdown are Spring trees

on the brink of flowering.
God, in his incalculable efforts,
is making yet another attempt
to free you from unlived living.

Say yes to the solid toehold offered.
Speak deep secrets to Him
directly or to a trusted person.
Be very honest as He defrosts them.

Those antique statues of bitter ice
housing regret and undealt emotions
are thriving wounds thought dead
in the dungeon, scarcely scabbed over,

bleeding from the mouth of the stream's
large library of justifications, checking you
out of todayness. Be brave as dungeon
doors open.

Hidden hurt's harrowing hold will cease.
Wounds will rise on outflux of balsamic
waters, break surface after years a glacier,
lose power. Allow it. External expression

to remove the dark distance from
His restorative arms.
A sure sunrise will surround you.

360 Degrees

                    To what degree
Are you willing
                    To see beyond
                            the borders of idiosyncrasy?

Are you willing
                    To allow accessibility
                    To thwart vulnerabilities
                          exacting eye
                              dictating safety
                    To authenticities denied?

Are you willing
                    To risk honesty
                    To foster faith
                    To foresee the seedling
                          that will shoot
                    To liberty?

Are you willing?

Why Wait?

to say you love

to give someone a sincere compliment

to make that phone call you need to make

act on that kind thought....

Tomorrow

no guarantee

Today

a diamond.

Say Goodbye To Distractions

Solitude is as needful to the imagination as society is wholesome for the character.
- James Russel Lowell

Breathe deeply. Allow words to spill from your mind
into your fingertips. Write or type them.
No need to be organized or elaborate
but do so if you choose.

Send them to a private space and command them
to stay as you would a petulant child
to her room with nothing to do but endeavor
to change her attitude.

Trust this time to sit in quietness. Questions may arise.
"How is my day? What's on my mind?
What do I want to change, keep, leave behind?
Are there gemstones or screams trapped inside?"

Give answers an outlet.
No set time, no deadline, no need to share.
You can rip the paper or hit delete
but get the words out first.

You may be peacefully surprised to find
that written words, like midwives,
will encourage you to push through
and find your hidden truth.

Present, Quiet, Fully Conscious

Go where you can
distance the door
to the world.

Just being
present
quiet
fully conscious.

Listening
not accomplishing,
if only for five, ten minutes
maybe fifteen?

Becoming
harmonious and easeful,
blazing beyond perfect
stems that hem you

a realigned vessel
awakened
laughing.

From Her Labyrinth

*Sing so loud that the music drowns out the sounds of naysayers.
One day they'll be singing your song.* - JaTawny Muckelvane Chatom

A naysayer nests in my breast
slithers in my blood

flays creativity, steals pleasure
dines under a dark sun

this irrational taskmaster
sounds from her labyrinth

makes fat, self-doubt
spews rotten crumbs

from her brazen lips
caws at my collapse.

Forget the Old Song

Take your greatest concern
and abandon it to Jesus.
Ask, beg if needed, for the gift
of childlike confidence in Him.
Re-entrust the situation.

Surrender the past to His mercy,
the future to His providence.
His grace, new each day,
cannot be accrued beforehand.
Trust it will be there when you need it.

Be faithful to your call.
Accept mystery.
Some things are not
meant to be explained.
Believing is a higher order than seeing.

Work on your own conversion.
Break the inertia. Forget the old song.
Walk with naked feet
over fallen rose branches
unharmed.

Scent   The Invitation

Stop and see

busy persons take notice

of a rose's hurting bloom

dismissed by blanketed

eyes alight with myth

educing guarantee

that haste is superior

to bending

to blatant beauties

left wilting in cold crowds

issuing fragrant bidding

in dying decree

blossoms

gone

before long.

Hands Hold Voice

Awakened
unbenumbed and bestrirring
halted hands long-drowned at sea
find their voice again in waves reaching
imagination's longing

as they twirl with new-found pliability
in the arms of the ocean
as they feel parameters unfurling

as they splash onto sand in artful motion
as words pulse pages in verse.
Musicality bursts onto canvases,
bold brush strokes

as they birth song into seas ,
vowing not to forsake authenticity
or risk sinking.

Found Fortune

Your heart and my heart are very old friends. - Rumi

What fuels fervor so fortunately as free time fitted with favored friends?

Airborne

Is There No Way Out Of The Mind? - Sylvia Plath

Rising to a distant place
Floating on a cloud of quiet
Longing for rest, fulfilled

Dangling thoughts in the silence
Exploring their efforts to speak
    to become ordered yet
Welcoming their disarray

Discovering how to dance solo
Relinquishing expectations to produce
Closing eyes
Awakening

Descending
Falling into life's mind-trap
Forming a union with time
    organized,
 Desiring to be.

Night Blooming

Close your mind

let sleep be sleep

infinite possibilities align

under moon's bedsheet

Dreams break open

touch Mercury's heartbeat

when dimness vicinities dawn

awaken a sea rolling.

Brimming Bouquet

Make an Angelica of love,

one that seeks not to be grand.

May it glorify with its blossoming,

drink of living water,

a chalice of choice wine.

Harvested

Thank you
to the one
who planted the orange tree

the one who picked
its fruit from the grove

the one
who transported it
who stocked
the store's shelf

for raindrops
sunlight   soil   air   space
weather that cooperated

for hands
to feel   to hold
fingers to peel
sense of smell

for tongue to savor
vitamins oxygenating body

headspace to meditate
on breaths between bites.

The Quality of Mercy

That gentle hallowed rain

said to be abstract

is not to be abstract at all.

It has arms as real

as Daddy's tight hug

and a heart softer than

mama's lips on my forehead.

Out Of My Limitations Words Cascade

sprinting over fences

and slippery stones

I write on ardent blank pages

sparking summertime thoughts.

More Than Hours

Happiness quite unshared can scarcely be called happiness; it has no taste.
- Charlotte Brontë

Honeyed flames spilling from my fingertips rain joy that lasts more than hours.

Brought To Remember

As we have loved... - Mary Oliver

You don't choose your family. They are God's gift to you as you are to them.
- Desmond Tutu

Dad: Your Time, Your Patience, Your Rocklike Love

Come to the edge, He said... They said, We are afraid. Come to the edge, He said. They came. He pushed them and they flew. - Guillaume Apollinaire

We entertain ourselves
doing ordinary things on our father-daughter
weekend at Orange Beach.

We search for seashells,
sidestep stinging nettles,
enjoy favorite restaurants and watch boats
come and go under Perdido Pass.

We catch sunsets and moonglow
with cocktails in hand as you
recount old and new happenings ending
with apropos quotes as you love to do.

Listening and laughing, I enjoy your wit
and relish life-lessons you continue to teach
except those when I was a teen
and thought I knew everything.

I pass this wisdom
to my three grown girls
from their grandfather,

a consummate Southern gentleman,
a God-fearing lover of people, poetry,
bridge playing, long conversations
and Alabama football,

a dapper dresser with a riot of tight gray curls
I used to pull to your shoulders
when young and bored on car trips
then watch them spring into tight tunnels.

My love for you is immense, extraordinary.

Ode to Mother
(Claudia Slade Lindsey Methvin)

Grief is a pain so great that it is almost a physical presence inside you.
- Caroline Myss

Taking your last breath
I lie beside you in bed
weeping, praying, placing
a final earthly kiss on your cheek
knowing we will meet again

envisioning elation felt
as your soul enters Heaven
as you waltz with Jesus
to His Christmas Cantata

as I'm certain God chose
the merriest season
to carry you home
as your life revealed
a heart conformed to His

as You lived by The Golden Rule
as the fruit of the Spirit you exuded
as your voice echoes inside me
as I aspire to be like you

Remembering Mother

The empty space where

the grand oak once stood

is lonely

Most passersby give no thought

to the natural occurrence

in the woods

But I am brought to remember

our talks, our walks

have been interrupted

and my heart

lies open.

Missing Mother

        The sky is moving
     the day
  allowing…

        The breeze is playing
     the treetops
  showering…

        The rose is flaunting
     the marigold
  taunting…

        My heart is towering
     I miss you
longingly…

Mother's Last Words

    Her tongue slow
      to unfold
       utters

        I

love
      love
              love
you

       you

Then we hug.

The last words I hear
Mother say
before Alzheimer's
stole her speech.

Mourning the Death of Deep Conversation (A Conversation with Myself)

Claudia Lindsey Methvin Hannahan, **what** is that tight fist in your inner cellar you say you cannot escape? What is the emptiness that causes headaches, that craves the comforting taste of extravagant conversation, the radical awareness of His Presence, the sort that **unfetters** cobwebs, **dissects** thoughts, and pulls up roots, the sort where two people feast on uninterrupted time together.

Claudia Lindsey, we are focused and present. Listen. Learn. Love in safe share. I becomes we, we becomes all; we **go deep**. Everyone belongs. We pray, ponder, and peek at how God works in our lives.

Lindsey, **let go ego**. Savor precious present. Feast on daily bread like fish racing to the fish-feeder, like cows running to hay on the back of the four wheeler, like Bella, our Beagle, eternally starving.

Linds, listen. We'll clean our plates. Taste today. Enlightenment lands on our platters as if it's our birthday. Contemplation is our demeanor; we reason together. We are soul companions. We **ponder** our **purpose**, free of illusions. We know who we are.

Lindsey Lou, Mother is calling. What are you starving for, she asks? She knows when we die to ourselves, epiphany is born. **Resurrect life's meaning**. Deep discussion about what matters truly.
Serve others. Endeavor to live on purpose. Make a difference.
Be filled with fruit. Taste and tell. Pass the bread basket.

I Drown in Blue Dawn

> Daughter resting in blue sea
> of Forget Me Nots
> Mother's beloved hue

I stroll through the woods beside a still lake
pondering that death is to arrive-
that separation cannot erase memories
of our time together,

that the glossy magnolia leaf-shine
under a cerulean lamp at morning tide
inspires my art--

a gentle presence redirects my footing
and places my hand in the knotty fingers
of a mossy oak pointing through foliage

to wild blue beauties befriending my foray.
Mesmerized by spring's sapphire showstoppers
beckoning with tiny golden eyes my haven.

Homeplace

"Keep this land together." Papa Slade said in a hand-written letter. This land off Highway 43, north of McIntosh, Alabama was purchased in 1862. Here, three generations of Slades gather biannually for our property meeting and a day of family bonding.

This land is where ancestry talk lingers in the dining room long after lunch, where actualized nostalgia wraps around acreage like an old thick quilt, where homeplace walks, timber management talks, a stroll inside the restored one-room school house replete with authentic desks, books, chalkboard and other relics used from 1900 to 1915 are cherished.

This land is where The Tombigbee and Three Rivers Lake meet, where prolific hunting seasons and year-round fishing provides pleasure, where Mother grew up with two brothers until she left for Mobile to live with Aunt Cile and attend Murphy High School, where deer would come when summoned to feed from opened palms.

This land is where my family of five would delight in each Christmas after a five-hour drive when my brothers and I were young children, is the place where Mama instilled in us a love for her homestead and family, where her nightgown got entangled in a wall-heater when she was around age eight, and grandmother, we fondly called Dama, snuffed out the flames with her genteel hands, never to play the piano again-

Here, where we watched sheep being sheared and played in the grove among horses, cows, dogs, and peacocks, where I revisit buried fear as I am brought to remember myself running as a child from an angry bull to safety onto a gargantuan fallen Southern Oak.

This is where my grandfather, Judge Lindsey, would yell from his comfortable chair to Mama, "Sista, remove these loud children from this room. I can't see nor hear the five o'clock news."

This is where I join aged interlacing threads of shock and sadness woven throughout the house's foundation as I am brought to remember Mama telling me the tragedy of her youngest brother Jimmy, who at age nine, fell from his horse to his death.

Here is where Lasses, the caretaker, would sleep in his one-room home behind the Big House, enter the kitchen early each morning with a mammoth smile and a mild demeanor to prepare a country breakfast feast complete with eggs he had taken me to collect from the hen house.

This land is a part of me I call home; now bittersweet because Mama's not physically here, yet this is where the arable soil's ruddy cheeks release a welcoming sigh to Slade heirs bodying forth long ago times.

Moving Mother and Daddy
Out of Our Childhood Home of 51 Years

Hidden emotions awaken,
magnified in moonlight
arriving at breakneck speed
dodging mind-traffic
muddled in dream.

Traveling on the tarmac
of memory,
I lie breathless
as the jet stream passes
and I lift my pen.

On a Field of Fresh Clover
(For Patrick)

The Alabama River glistened before us
on that warm April afternoon, 2018.
Beesong was our music,
rainshine our cover.

We stood on a field of fresh clover
in the shadow of a sweetgum tree
beaming as we discussed
our three daughters,

my ambereyes raised to your skyblueirises.
I don't know how long we held hands,
Bella, our beloved Beagle
breathing between us.

Husband-Best Friend

When we first met in college you were wearing
a light green shirt that turned your blue eyes chartreuse
and driving a red Camero headed to a different party.
I thank The Giver you turned your car around
and followed my friends and me instead.

A week later it took me over an hour to ask you
to my sorority crush party. What if you said no?
You said "yes. "

That's when we began five years of dating
and in thirty of marriage, you've stayed steady
 as a stone throughout the decades.

When I hear your uproarious laugh as you
watch a favorite sitcom,
when yelling with me like crazy people
when we watch Alabama football,
 Roll Tide Roll.

When I hear the fervor in your voice as you

swap hunting-fishing stories with your friends,

my smile broadens.

When you look at me now as you did

when we were first married

and have always loved me just as I am,

I realize how fortunate I am.

Thank you my most marvelous man

for your upstanding character and firm faith,

for being a remarkable Father to our three daughters

for giving me strength by believing in me at my best-worst,

for your desire to protect me from life's hardships,

for not getting too mad when I can't balance

the checkbook and chuckling when the chicken is overcooked.

When each day moves into tomorrow

I found a man stronger than anyone I know.*

* *Perfect* - Ed Sheeran and Beyoncé

As Eventide Approaches
(For Patrick)

Your strong hand cuddling my waist,

our naked toes tenderly touching as

eventide approaches our stilled boat

in this, our small segment of Heaven,

Little Dauphin Island Bay.

The most famous star shouts Hallelujah

in her best western dress as she sinks

golden on her fiery stage,

spilling her tonic of romance and burgundy

over coastal waters of The Mississippi Sound.

In great glory and grace,

she greets the famished waves

stirring the skyscape into God's chosen palette,

her pupils, purpling pools of perfection,

gifting thoughts feathers.

Her lashes, lengthening swaths of electricity,

gifting observers inspiration.

Her hair, awash in hot hues,

falls through glossy clouds

pretty poses

piercing violet-blue,

melding crimson- coral

into an orangy overdose,

gifting ribbons of delightful rose,

gifting meaning to ordinary life

as she escorts revival to our four eyes

as full as a city beside its broken levy,

our two hearts loving each other

over a quarter of a century

as we marvel at light at play.

Our road, not without troubles.

Our faith, not without fright.

Silently we surrender with the sun

as day and darkness

briefly brush us.

Home for A Swift Visit
(For Mary Lindsey)

Before starting summer work,
having completed your second year of college,
you bring me coffee in bed and climb in.

You lay your head on my shoulder and tell me
you've missed me. I wrap my arm around you
hoping you feel my heart's glee.

We indulge in reminiscence.
I think back to the morning you were born,
my happiness absolute as I cradled you,

thanked God for your birth, prayed for His protection,
guidance and that you keep close to Him.
I touch your soft cheek, grateful for the gracious

young lady you are. You remind me of our made-up
song, "Your're my snuggle, snuggle, snuggle,
snuggle queen, whoo, whoo."

We sing it. Complete with hands romping
in air like we did when I put you to bed
before your preteens arrived.

We giggle and gab. I whisper in your ear,
"Thank you for making me a Mother twenty- three
years ago, my adored sunflower:

beautiful, brilliant, crowd- pleaser
loyal, strong, spirit-lifter.
My joy, loving you."

Celebrate Claudia

Remember, "There is no one alive who is youer than you." - Dr. Seuss

+++

Remember when I would tuck you in at night and you would hold me so tight repeating, "I'll neeeever let you go. I'll neeeever let you go."

+++

Remember the note you wrote me when you were eight:
"Dear Mom, are we still friends? I am sorry about what happened today and I'll try not to do it again. Love CCH." Remember you always go to my heart to get out of trouble.

+++

Remember, Claudia, also this year, you killed your first deer. Dad was so proud of you. And ya'll would turn up the volume and sing, "It's a Great Day to Be Alive." This beginning a fun, new tradition.

+++

And remember the ceramic redbird you made me at that boring summer camp I made you attend in 2008. You knew The Gift of the Redbird is one of my favorite books. The redbird is a sign that God is present. Each day is a gift. Claudia, have you forgiven me?

+++

Remember the free hug and I will not whine for a day coupon books you gave me when you were ten. And the scrapbook you made for my birthday when you were eleven ending with "Just don't ever forget me."

+++

Remember last Easter I asked how many bucks you had killed and you said "twenty-one bucks. Twenty-one bucks by the time I'm 21, my goal. I reached it a few months ago."

+++

My Darling Claudia, Remember you are radiant outwardly and within, genuine, kind, competent, sensitive to other's needs, grounded in your Christian faith, a devoted sister, daughter, friend with a Mother who adores you.

Happy Twenty-First Birthday, Claudi, April 29, 2017
I'll neeeeeeever let you go.

Blessed by Grace

Two ecstatic sisters, ages five and seven
wanted to whisk you home from the hospital
the second you were born
with that easy-going personality

and innate social finesse
a constant smile and rosy cheeks.
Without you, Baby Grace,
our family wouldn't be complete.

You sang the day you started talking,
danced the day you started walking,
wrote songs not long after learning to form sentences,
performing for your charmed parents.

"Daddy, please, please, please can you move
your office from Mobile to Los Angeles
so I can be on the Disney Channel
and be famous like Hannah Montana."

Tap, jazz, ballet, hip-hop classes ruled
your nights and days. Solo, duo, trio routines
and Center Stage elaborate costumes made
for competitive dancing,

trophies, medals, ribbons won,
then on to cheerleading, tennis,
not for a second forsaking
hunting and deep-sea fishing.

My dear Sweet Sixteen
considerate, smart, warm-hearted
I miss you already in two years
when you leave home for college

and I love you more than
you'll ever want to hear.
What pleasure to watch you grow and learn.
We bask in your gentle spirit.

Mother's Advice on Choosing Close Friends
(For my daughters)

A good friend loves at all times. - Proverbs 17:17

Does she expand your spirit,
understand your deepest needs,
speak hard truths with encouragement
even when you don't want to hear it?

Does she give solid love, solid support?
Is she trustworthy and attentive?
Does she share your aches, share your joys,
practice the art of listening?

Is she unselfish, slow to anger?
Does she treat your burdens as her own?
Is she spiritually connected, a granter of forgiveness?
Does she help you be your better self?

Are you a friend one seeks to have?
A divine gift to laugh with, cry with
have fun with, just be with?
No agenda necessary.

Could This Be True?
(For Tom)

Though we live in different cities
we visit or talk by phone about life's goings--on
and how God provides for our families.

Though we fought as siblings do when growing up
we had fun, looked after each other
and kept each other's confidences.

Though I've not forgotten the night you botched
my over-sprayed hair and makeup
when I had prepared for hours
minutes before a first date rang the doorbell
and I cried angry waterfalls;

day after, I cried loving tears when you
fell off your racing go-cart onto a gravel road
as I helped Mother nurse your gross wounds.

Though you still tease me and declare
I never stop talking, "Could this be true?"
I allow it because I adore spending time with you
my successful, humble, live-your-religion big brother,
constant helper of the less fortunate.

Though I tremble to think,
"What would I do, how would I cope without
our close brother-sister friendship?"

Unbroken
(For Bob)

Childhood memories climb my thoughts.
You, age eleven, zooming on your bicycle
five miles to the hospital to see your big sister.
I, having been hit by a car. No one home to drive you.

And untold times I made you play store and school
until you were old enough to rebel and escape my grasp.
I apologize.

"Hurry up. Let's go." You would whisper each Sunday
after we finished a pot roast lunch with rice, gravy
green beans and Gram's delicious homemade biscuits.
We would clean dishes with haste and fly out the door
running up and down Woodland Drive yelling to friends "It's time."
Gram would be waiting in her car to take the neighborhood
children to the Zippy Mart to stock up on candy,
returning home with sugary lips and large grins.

And do you remember when I threw your weight bench
across the room? You had placed it in the downstairs closet
on top of my winter clothes. Again, I apologize.

I cherish our unbroken sibling bond,
our family get-togethers and the brotherly love
I detect in your voice when you phone
from Birmingham to chat.

You, a flourishing family man of upstanding character,
a practitioner of your faith
with the innate ability to make others laugh.

I am proud to call you brother.

A Sweet Retreat

April knock-out rose
memories of Grandmother
fall into teacup

Indulge in bright-bursting teacups, inhale the fragrant family
of knock-out roses gathering in bunched beds flowering
often ignored candy apple red-heads, doubly
dressed in romantic clothing, spicing
the backyard from April to first
frost. A continual breakfast
in Mobile, Alabama,
manna to feed
on and on
and on.

Dear Catherine

I love your seafood gumbo
homemade soup and fried chicken,
the rapport we share
and our valued conversations

my husband you nurtured
a man of principal,
the doting grandmother you are
to our three children.

"Can I pick up from carpool,
take the girls to get ice cream?
I'll keep the baby tonight
so you can get some sleep."

Your prayerful practices
and infectious faith
inspire me to emulate
your excellent example.

Your selfless heart and helpful
hands bolster our community.
I love and appreciate you
Mother-in law, friend.

Playing Field

We run along the winding muddied road
down a golden sycamore row
past ragweed and broom
sage forgotten

pass wild red roses
bursting   bragging   bombarding
the bald eagle's eye
merry-go-rounding

onto a canary citrus blanket
stopping   stepping   sliding
stinging   scenting   snailing
sole and paw.

We gallop as early morning Christmas
children, Bella's collar jingling at my feet
two heart's hammering
amid sapid cedars

onto a playground of doe and fawn feeding
bustling   blazing   browsing
beside nine point
discarded antlers

as knees knock grass we begin
praising   praying   pardoning
curiosity playing with laughter
as fresh friends gather

rounding   racing   reigning
we prance together.

A Day That Can Be

Sunlight shatters blue satin as we soak in music,
four daughters and a son of Mobile Bay with work behind us,
fun upon us, laughter with us, oil rigs near us

with cargo ships from faraway places waiting in the channel
to enter port. Dolphins sky-hop, ling surface, salty sprays matt hair
and shower tanned bodies: the air full of love, gulls, pelicans.

We cross the mouth of Mobile Bay pass Fort Morgan Peninsula
down the Intercoastal Waterway to lunch in Gulf Shores,
meet friends in Orange Beach.

This moment, this morning a thousand kisses deep.*

A Thousand Kisses Deep - Leonard Cohen*

Dauphin Island Family Morning

This Dauphin Island morning,
warm and cloudless greets
three daughters arriving for the weekend;
even the sting ray hiding near our small beach
plays without restraint.
He risks being seen by his arch enemy
as he swings his flappers to the sweet beat
of a red-winged blackbird's whistle,

somehow lifting his flat body close
to Pass Drury Bay's surface.
His eyes protrude above water
like the sail of a submarine and glimmer
as he watches gulls-go-round with Bella, our Beagle
the girls catching sun,
gabbing and giggling as they did
when they were young.

Patrick tinkers with the Contender to get it ride-ready.
I prepare snacks and sandwiches.
Soon we head out through Billy Goat Hole,
pass the Coast Guard Building and Little Dauphin Island
into the grand Gulf of Mexico to catch
this year's scant two-per-person
limit of red snapper,
sting rays swimming in our wake.

A Mix of Memory

Something that more or less kills me with delight. - Mary Oliver

Tuesday lunches with my father,
hard rain on a tin roof,
an excellent glass of cabernet,
Grace's hand on my cheek.

Unexpected Happy Birthday wishes,
roadside flowering pear trees,
wind as waterfall in loblolly pines,
Miami Beach with Mary Lindsey.

Church bells' noontime song,
an Eagles concert with Claudia,
sounds of children playing in the schoolyard,
a cleared conscious.

Lake Rabun summers and Atlanta Thanksgivings
with Martha and Tom;
blackbird praises from a concrete angel,
poetry in the Botanical Gardens.

Low-tide beaches, deep-sea fishing
with Grammy and Poppa;
Mardi Gras barn parties and Mardi Gras balls
with Bernice and Billy.

Lively destinations with sorority sisters,
festive get-togethers with childhood pals,
coffee-wine-laughter with Mobile dear friends:
Patrick beside me.

On Sand Island

an extravaganza of amazing athletes
gather flapping and yapping under cumulus clouds.

Dolphin calves play-fight in the deep around their mother.
Our young daughters callisteia in sand.

Patrick casts a hopeful line.
Hermit crabs splash, hide, and parade into shallow ripples.

Boats with redwhiteblue flags anchor near shore.
Friends crowd the dim-day beach.

Fireworks open night's door to childlike
astonishment longtime locked in my memory.

Acknowledgments

Many, many thanks to Sue Walker,
acclaimed author, mentor and friend.

Many thanks to Jenni Krchak book designer, editor and artist.

I would like to express my great appreciation to my writing group
at the Mobile Botanical Gardens - Writers In Nature
Shannon Brown, Marbury Buckhaults, Gail Gehlken,
Lisadawn Hamilton, Mavis Jarrell, Catherine Hall Kiser,
Winn Levert, Sheri Mullin, Derek Norman, Joan Peterson,
Roz Rountree, Dr.Maryella Sirmon,
Carolee Scott, and Melissa Wold.

www.ingramcontent.com/pod-product-compliance
Lightning Source LLC
Chambersburg PA
CBHW030444300426
44112CB00009B/1151